Especially for Grand- parents

when was the last time...

This Book Is a Gift for

_____

From

_____

Especially for Grand-parents

when was the last time...

MICHAEL A. CAMPION, PH.D.
with photographs by Wilmer Zehr

Bethany Fellowship INC.
MINNEAPOLIS, MINNESOTA 55438

***Especially for
Grandparents***

Copyright © 1980
Bethany Fellowship, Inc.
All rights reserved

Published by Bethany Fellowship, Inc.
6820 Auto Club Road
Minneapolis, Minnesota 55438

Printed in the United States of America

ISBN 0-87123-141-7

The fifty key behaviors
selected for
Especially for Grandparents
were chosen from hundreds of
sincere comments of concern,
joy, and good memories submitted
by grandparents of all ages.

This book is an effort to help develop and sustain an attitude which expresses those special memories that last forever in grandchildren's hearts.

It is also a reminder of the importance of putting life into the perspective of eternity—considering each day what is done and said of lasting value.

Life is a wonderful gift. If one lives to be very old, let him rejoice in every day of life; but let him also remember that eternity still stretches out ahead. The writer of Ecclesiastes puts it this way: "It is a wonderful thing to be alive! If a person lives to be very old, let him rejoice in every day of life, but let him also remember that eternity is far longer, and that everything down here is futile in comparison" (11: 7, 8, TLB).

The true legacy that Grandma and Grandpa can give is a host of good memories that come from a relationship of sharing love with their grandchildren. We hope this book will help review and remind of those special times that build good memories. So ask yourself . . .

when was the last time...

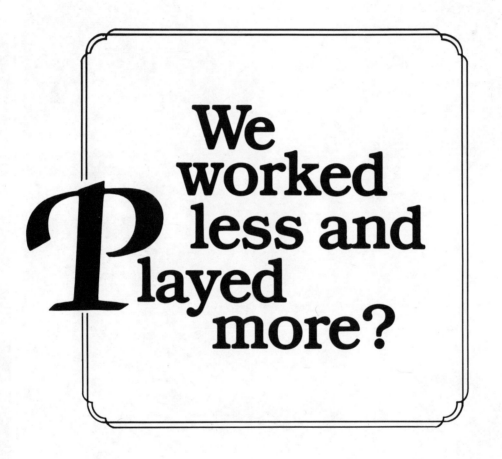

We worked **P**less and layed more?

We
were not
resentful
about
the
High cost
of living?

We Prayed with our grand-children?

We Watched the sky and found pictures in the clouds?

We did not criticize our children's efforts at being parents?

We Shared our knowledge and wisdom with our grand-children?

We showed Affection when we saw our grand-children?

We Disciplined the grand-children?

We were willing to Change?

We took
the grand-
children
to a
Restaurant?

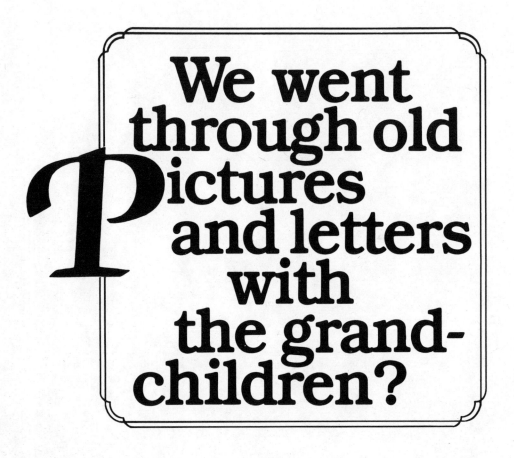

We went through old Pictures and letters with the grand-children?

We checked
to see if the
Presents we
planned
to give
were O.K.?

We dried the grand-children's Tears and said everything would be all right?

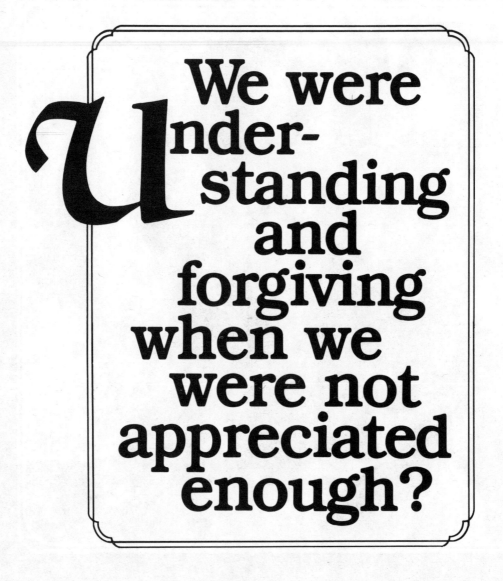

We were Understanding and forgiving when we were not appreciated enough?

We had family
Get-togethers
and sing-a-longs?

We had a
Christmas
Party for
the whole
family?

We let the grand-children Look around in cupboards and trunks?

We bought our grand-children thoughtful Gifts instead of sending them money?

SELF-EVALUATION FOR GRANDPARENTS

The following inventory is a self-evaluation of your relationship as grandparents to each other and the grandchildren. Circle the number in front of the statement which best estimates your frequency of doing that particular behavior. For example: 0, 1, 2, 3, 4, WE THANKED GOD FOR ALL OUR BLESSINGS. If you thanked God for your blessings one time in the last twelve months, circle the 1. If you have thanked Him several times this week, circle the 4.

Respond in like manner to all 50 statements, and then total your score. If some behavior is not applicable to your situation, give yourself a total of 4 points. Have a friend of yours who is a grandparent, or several friends who are grandparents, take the inventory and compare the results. For your convenience, you may wish to record your scores below with the date and re-examine yourself once or twice a year and measure your progress. Now go back over your self-evaluation and pick one behavior that you would like to do with or for your grandchildren this week and make a real effort to do it.

Date and result of self-evaluation:

Date _____ Score _____

Date _____ Score _____

Date _____ Score _____

Date _____ Score _____

Date _____ Score _____

SELF-EVALUATION

Circle Response:
TIMES
LAST
12 MOS.

Rate yourself and compare your score with a friend's results.

	Or More	When was the last time...
0 1 2 3	4	We talked about how GOOD we felt?
0 1 2 3	4	We showed love to each other in front of the grandchildren?
0 1 2 3	4	We took the grandchildren to the zoo?
0 1 2 3	4	We wrote letters to the grandchildren?
0 1 2 3	4	We worked less and played more?
0 1 2 3	4	We were not resentful about the high cost of living?
0 1 2 3	4	We prayed with our grandchildren?
0 1 2 3	4	We watched the sky and found pictures in the clouds?
0 1 2 3	4	We held our grandchildren, hugging and kissing them?
0 1 2 3	4	We did not criticize our children's efforts at being parents?
0 1 2 3	4	We made homemade ice cream?
0 1 2 3	4	We shared our knowledge and wisdom with our grandchildren?
0 1 2 3	4	We were content with our age?
0 1 2 3	4	We had time to listen to our grandchildren?
0 1 2 3	4	We shared our faith in God with our grandchildren?
0 1 2 3	4	We showed affection when we saw our grandchildren?
0 1 2 3	4	We took our grandchildren on an outing?
0 1 2 3	4	We disciplined the grandchildren?
0 1 2 3	4	We were willing to change?
0 1 2 3	4	We babysat with the grandchildren?
0 1 2 3	4	We did not count on just the family for our total social life?
0 1 2 3	4	We wanted the grandchildren to visit for a few days?
0 1 2 3	4	We took the grandchildren to a restaurant?
0 1 2 3	4	We laughed and laughed and laughed?

0 1 2 3 4	We went through old pictures and letters with the grandchildren?
0 1 2 3 4	We baked cookies?
0 1 2 3 4	We checked to see if the presents we planned to give were O.K.?
0 1 2 3 4	We helped someone older than ourselves?
0 1 2 3 4	We thanked God for all of our blessings?
0 1 2 3 4	We were proud of the grandchildren and let them know it?
0 1 2 3 4	We visited a new place?
0 1 2 3 4	We dried the grandchildren's tears and said everything would be all right?
0 1 2 3 4	We gave our love equally to all of our grandchildren?
0 1 2 3 4	We were understanding and forgiving when we were not appreciated enough?
0 1 2 3 4	We had family get-togethers and sing-a-longs?
0 1 2 3 4	We didn't take life so seriously?
0 1 2 3 4	We accepted our grandchildren the way they are?
0 1 2 3 4	We had a Christmas party for the whole family?
0 1 2 3 4	We enjoyed an outdoor sport?
0 1 2 3 4	We read stories to the grandchildren?
0 1 2 3 4	We worked on recording the family history?
0 1 2 3 4	We relaxed more with our grandchildren?
0 1 2 3 4	We made the grandchildren feel special?
0 1 2 3 4	We read to the grandchildren from the family Bible?
0 1 2 3 4	We told stories of when we were young?
0 1 2 3 4	We attended our grandchildren's school activities?
0 1 2 3 4	We let the grandchildren look around in cupboards and trunks?
0 1 2 3 4	We remembered the grandchildren's birthdays?
0 1 2 3 4	We bought our grandchildren thoughtful gifts instead of sending them money?
0 1 2 3 4	We laid the groundwork on which our grandchildren can build good memories?

TOTAL